THE BIG LEADER LEADERSHIP EXPERT

THE BIG LEADER LEADERSHIP EXPERT

THE BIG LEADER LEADERSHIP EXPERT

INDEX

Chapter 1: The Leadership Gene

Chapter 2: Becoming a Great Leader

Chapter 3: Emotional Intelligence in Leadership

Chapter 4: Building Successful Teams and Relationships

Chapter 5: Managing Difficult Times and Conflict Effectively

 THE BIG LEADER LEADERSHIP EXPERT

Chapter 1: The Leadership Gene

The issue of leadership and genetics has been discussed and researched since the concept of leadership was created. Research efforts have focused on exploring the link between the two. Are leaders born or made?

This will sound like a cliché, but so far, genetics is still considered a major factor in determining the formation of leaders. But not everyone thinks the same way. There may be some truth to it, but factors such as experiences and social dynamics are also important in leadership.

There is no single factor that determines a person's ability to lead.

Each factor is important to some extent.

Some scientists have a strong feeling about genetic and biological factors and their relationship to leadership. The interest in the link between genetics and leadership is triggered by people from the same family taking leadership positions in society.

The Kennedys and the Bush family are two examples. More than genetics, science is also concerned with the biological and physical traits that leaders possess. There are studies that show how genetics contribute to a person's physiological and psychological functions. These will eventually affect a person's cognitive and behavioral traits, which determine whether a person is fit for leadership. Hormones and chemical changes in the body affect a person's cognitive functioning, a very important aspect of leadership.

When it comes to leadership, it is always a question of nature versus nature.

However, the two are intertwined and cannot be separated.

Leadership cannot be discussed without considering both at the same time.

An example would be the chemical and hormonal changes in the body that will affect a person's disposition. Disposition will affect attitude and behavior, which are huge factors in leadership.

An example would be a person suffering from a bipolar disorder.

People with bipolar disorder tend to show very dramatic mood swings, easily going from euphoria to depression. There are several causes of bipolar disorder, including neurotransmitters that are inherited. Your bipolar tendencies will affect your personality, which will affect your leadership style. This does not mean that bipolar people are not capable leaders. In fact, it has been reported that the world's greatest leaders were bipolar (e.g., Abraham Lincoln, Winston Churchill, and Napoleon Bonaparte). However, their dramatic mood swings can have negative effects on their leadership and on establishing trust with their followers.

As already mentioned, external (parenting) factors in leadership cannot be ruled out. The Kennedys may be a family of leaders, but it must be kept in mind that the members are exposed to the same environment and values. They are exposed to almost the same group of people and circumstances. Even if genetics played an important role in their leadership streak, you can't take away the fact that they thrive in a common environment. They were exposed to the same kind of experiences and were raised by the same group of people who also share the same values. They are also bound to develop similar views on important issues and perhaps develop the same leadership style.

There are certain environments that are conducive to shaping leaders. The environment plays a very important role in the formation of a person's ideals, opinions and values. If young children are raised by parents who promote pro-social behavior, children will grow up to overcome irrational aggression and form healthy relationships with their peers. Role models count heavily in the formation of a person's leadership traits. When a child is surrounded by people with strong leadership attributes, the child is likely to absorb these attributes as well. Likewise, children surrounded by aggressive role models are more likely to be aggressive. Aggression and social skills are very important in leadership because to be an effective leader, the individual must be skilled in dealing with people. Leaders must establish a relationship with their colleagues

and subordinates.

In general, many leadership attributes are shaped by external factors. Even if it is claimed that leadership qualities are inherent in a person, the fact is that a person will continue to develop while he or she is alive. Some traits will be more developed by others. The person's attitude and personality will be influenced by the people around him. Other environmental factors that affect the person (e.g., the political atmosphere, economic conditions, life-changing events) will also determine the set of leadership traits he or she will possess. These are the formative experiences that can produce a leader.

Related to the formative experiences are the social dynamics to which the person is subject. For example, a given woman may have good social skills and a strong conviction, but her leadership qualities may not shine to their fullest extent if she is in a society where men are always considered the alpha figure. She may have the leadership potential, but if she thinks that men are always the legitimate leader, she may not be able to exhibit her leadership qualities to the fullest. The position in the family is also an example of the impact of social dynamics on leadership. Many first-born sons are often molded into leaders, although not all turn out to be good leaders.

Social dynamics are huge factors to some extent, similar to genetics and formative experiences. All three contribute to the development of a leader.

Some people may or may not have inherent leadership qualities, but experiences and relationships in life will affect a person's attitude.

Leadership qualities can be improved along the way. One's growth and development is certainly crucial in determining whether a person is fit to be a good leader.

Leadership styles vary but surely there must be common qualities that are common among great leaders. The attributes will measure whether the leader is doing a good job of serving his purpose.

Good leaders make a good first impression, not because of their skills and accomplishments. Although they are important, they are not the first things their people notice. People are attracted to leaders who ooze charisma. Charisma is a very attractive and inspiring trait that many great leaders possess. Identifying charisma is not easy because it cannot be articulated instantly. Charisma is a combination of many things - the way a person stands, moves, speaks, etc. Charismatic leaders have a vision (which will be discussed later) and the ability to articulate this vision. They must also have the ability to communicate with as many people as possible on an emotional level. Charismatic leaders make other people feel that they are able to relate to their situation, which is not very easy to do. Some people think that charisma is something that cannot be learned. For them, it is an inherent trait of every person. Either you have it or you don't. But modern thinkers do not agree with this mentality. They think that people can eventually learn to be charismatic, starting by being polite, courteous, and respectful. The point is to be "nice" and "friendly" to other people.

Charismatic leaders make other people feel that they are able not only to understand their situation, but also to relate to it. Not everyone has this ability but some are able to build charisma through age and time.

Leadership requires good people skills and sensitivity to the needs of others; it also builds blocks of charisma. After all, leadership would not exist if there were no people to lead. People's skills are built on the little things that people don't forget. For example, they appreciate that new acquaintances remember their names even if they have only met a few times. Charisma can eventually develop, as long as the person remembers to make other people feel comfortable and important.

Leadership begins with focus and vision. Leaders are not required to be all-knowing individuals, but they must be fully aware of the purpose and vision of the organization they are leading. Only by having a focus can a strong commitment and responsibility be formed. In addition, a leader must have the necessary competence in his or her field. Again, he or she need not be omniscient but requires sufficient knowledge in the field to make sound decisions.

No leader can endure the challenges of leadership without courage and strength of character. Of all the members of the organization, individuals who have leadership responsibilities cannot be influenced by anything or anyone. The leader must remember the purpose and vision of leadership in any decision-making process. The leader must have enough courage to stand up to anything or anyone that threatens to undermine that vision. Good leaders are also assertive in getting the job done and defending the organization's vision. He or she must be assertive enough to get people to do their jobs.

Good leaders must always be creative and resourceful because some situations will require them to think outside the box. Not all problems can be solved with textbook formulas and proven solutions. They must be courageous enough to move away from the conventional and find better ways of doing things.

Finally, a good leader must have a lot of passion and a sense of entitlement.

Leadership is not an easy feat, and if a leader tries to fulfill his duties without any passion, he may not be able to withstand challenges.

Leadership is a roller coaster experience and without passion, the leader may find it difficult to accept the difficulties. As for the sense of servitude, leaders cannot lead if they do not know what it is to serve. In addition, the purpose of the leader is to serve the organization and not just to give orders to people.

In the following chapters, we will delve into what makes a great leader and how status can be achieved, despite challenges. They will also help the reader to improve their current leadership skills and give them an idea of what awaits them as leaders.

Chapter 2: Becoming a Great Leader

Different leaders have different leadership styles, but they all need to learn to deal with human nature. This is not such an easy task considering the diversity of human nature. Great leaders have the ability to understand and work with different attitudes and personalities. To be an effective leader, one must develop fine social skills to relate to different types of people. People skills are crucial to empowering people, which is a primary task in leadership.

The author has chosen two main factors to discuss when it comes to empowerment. The first, empathy, is crucial for establishing open lines of communication between people in an organization. The second, motivation, is important for a team to be productive.

Empathy

A good leader must learn to empathize with the people he will work with. Empathy is a person's ability to show concern and understanding for the perspectives of others. Empathy should not be confused with sympathy. When you sympathize with others, you identify with them to the point of agreeing with the person's actions and plans. Empathy is not agreeing with a person. Empathy is being able to put yourself in another person's position and understand their thoughts and feelings.

Empathy does not mean agreeing with the person all the time. Empathy only involves understanding a person's point of view, even without giving advice. An effective leader needs to show empathy for other people.

It is crucial for building trust and strengthening relationships between people.

Productivity increases when people who work together share a healthy relationship. Empathy allows leaders to delve into the root cause of poor performance without being critical. By putting themselves in other people's shoes, they can make better changes in people's lives.

Empathy plays a very important role in empowering people. You don't have to agree with each and every point of view, but as a leader, you have to let the people around you realize that you understand them and know where they come from. When you approach people, don't let your thoughts be clouded by judgment right away. Showing empathy takes time because it is not always easy to understand why people think and feel the way they do.

By creating an environment where people feel comfortable expressing their opinions and thoughts, you can open yourself up to empathetic listening.

When talking to people, assure the speaker that you have their full attention. When people are about to confide in their problems, they feel more comfortable when they are assured of full attention. Listen to the speaker with an open mind and heart. Resist the temptation to judge him or her. This can be difficult at first because prejudice is almost inevitable, but the awareness that you have your own set of prejudices should help you avoid making judgments right away.

Avoid interrupting the speaker at all times, even if you are very upset about something. Don't be afraid of moments of silence. After the speaker has aired his thoughts, a brief pause will allow him to make sense of the situation and find his own solution. While the speaker is speaking, don't just listen to the words that come out of the mouth.

Give meaning to the emotions that accompany those words. More than words, you must be able to respond to the speaker's emotions. Ask relevant and sensible people to assure the speaker that they are interested and want to understand. Often, the speaker will be more comfortable with mere effort and gesture.

Motivation

Good leadership certainly involves superior motivational skills. Part of empowering people is being able to motivate them and get them moving. As a leader, it is important to know what motivates the people around you.

Needless to say, motivation goes hand in hand with empathy. Each person has different aspirations, dreams and interests. A good leader needs to take advantage of these to get each member of the group moving. People work for many reasons - income, personal fulfillment, growth, etc.

The leader should make an effort to talk to his or her team members individually to find out the source(s) of each person's motivation.

The common misconception of most leaders is that all team members are motivated by the same factors. Some members may share the same aspirations, but it does not always apply to everyone. Motivation can be very personal, making it difficult for inexperienced leaders to motivate each and every member of the team. When it comes to motivation, there is no such thing as "one size fits all.

The most common forms of motivation come from within, also known as internal motivation. Motivation comes from within, so leaders must maintain good lines of communication with their members to determine what motivates each team member. There are external factors that motivate a person, but these factors also have to harmonize with the internal motivational factors. In an office organization, the most common motivation would be salary, but good leaders know that something deeper than money motivates people. For example, why are people eager to earn money? Do they have a family to support? Are they saving for school? These motivations are something a leader can explore when talking personally with team members. People are motivated when they set very personal goals, apart from the goal to be achieved in the organization.

Human beings are not static. They thrive on constant challenge and encouragement. People must be assigned tasks that are increasingly difficult but still achievable. Their tasks should make them proud of themselves for having conquered challenges, whether small or large. Their tasks should be challenging but achievable. Be sure to give them constant feedback on their performance to give them a sense of accomplishment and a glimpse of their performance. One of the easiest sources of motivation is praise and recognition. People are more motivated to work when their achievements and efforts are recognized. However, you have to be careful with recognition. Recognize a person's achievements but do not do so in a way that causes envy and unhealthy competition among colleagues.

In relation to challenges, another source of motivation for many people is a task that quenches their thirst for knowledge. People need to be exposed to an environment where their curiosity is satisfied. Make their work environment more interesting to arouse curiosity and encourage learning as well.

A leader needs to constantly find out what motivates team members, as a group and as individuals. Good leaders don't just ask their members straight out what motivates them, because not everyone realizes it right away. Rather, good leaders must explore the values of each individual.

This gives them a more personal view of their lives, which will make it easier to find out what motivates them.

Allow each team member to set their own objectives, reminding them only occasionally to design their goals in line with the collective objective of the organization. This will give them a sense of control over their lives, which is a very important motivating factor for many people. Allowing them to set their own goals will give them a closer look at how their actions will affect their own objectives.

You can also use group work or teamwork as motivation factors. These are effective for people who like to work in groups. This will improve cooperation and relationships in the team. In addition, people are more likely to be motivated when they know that their own actions will affect the well-being of others. Cooperation will get more done and strengthen relationships between members.

Good leaders also know how to facilitate a competitive environment to motivate people. This tactic is used in almost any type of organization. Healthy competition will boost people's productivity because winning a competition gives a person a sense of accomplishment. Effective leaders will learn to use competition to motivate all team members.

As much as possible, leaders should encourage each member to compete against his or her own performance (even if they are competing with others). Leaders must also ensure that the competition is worthwhile even in the face of defeat. Leaders must be careful not to involve their team in a power struggle in which each member becomes a

THE BIG LEADER LEADERSHIP EXPERT

manipulator of others just to win a competition.

As mentioned above, different people have different motivations.

Therefore, a personal relationship must be cultivated with each employee to test the different factors that might motivate them. For example, some people are motivated by competition while others do not work well under pressure. It could be a "hit or miss" process but eventually, you will find each person's motivation. Keep the lines of communication open as to how each individual responds to motivational factors.

Get regular feedback and see that your team members are motivated.

It is also important to monitor your members for signs of demotivation. Clear the office space of any demotivating factors as much as possible. Maintain a healthy relationship between you and your members. You should also make sure that members maintain harmonious relationships with each other. People are more productive when they have a good relationship with their leaders and colleagues.

Finally, make sure that collective and individual goals are met.

In conclusion, leadership and empowerment of people is about understanding their deepest desires and helping them set goals that are also aligned with the collective goal of the organization. It is very important for a leader to reassure his or her members that they belong to an organization where even their personal goals and aspirations are highly valued.

Chapter 3: Emotional Intelligence in Leadership

Leadership cannot take place when the leader does not have enough emotional intelligence. A leader with sufficient emotional intelligence can overcome difficult leadership challenges that not many people can meet.

Studies in recent years indicate that people with high emotional intelligence are more adept at dealing with organizational conflict more effectively and quickly. Gone are the days when pure intellect was quickly equated with good leadership potential.

Emotional intelligence is a person's ability to recognize and deal with their own emotions as well as the emotions of others. Emotions can fluctuate due to hormonal changes, stress and unexpected situations that arise, but the right amount of emotional intelligence will help a person deal with emotional changes effectively.

People have different personalities, needs and preferences. Likewise, people have different ways of dealing with situations and expressing their emotions. Strong emotional intelligence is needed to deal with different personalities. People can feel different emotions at the same time and, in most cases, the challenge is to be able to deal with people's different emotions without causing conflict and straining relationships.

When a person has enough emotional intelligence, they are able to recognize their own emotions and how they affect the people around them.

Emotional intelligence is also a person's ability to understand how another person feels. It goes without saying that emotional intelligence is necessary in managing relationships.

In an organization, people who stay longer tend to have high emotional intelligence. In fact, high emotional intelligence is preferred to people with high IQs but low emotional intelligence.

It is easy to work with people of high emotional intelligence compared to those of low emotional intelligence. High emotional intelligence allows people to accomplish things by cultivating good relationships. They can keep their heads above water even in stressful situations. Emotionally intelligent people are not immune to agitation or stress. However, they can easily control the situation and seek a solution as calmly as possible. Therefore, they are forced to make good decisions because they manage their emotions well in the decision-making process.

Because emotionally intelligent people are sensible, they do not think too highly or too low of themselves. They know their strengths and weaknesses. They use their strengths when necessary, but do not show them in excess. Likewise, they are humble enough to look at themselves honestly and recognize their weaknesses. Emotionally intelligent

people do not easily succumb to criticism. They can take criticism objectively and use it to improve their performance.

Emotionally intelligent people are good team players because they focus solely on their own success. People with high emotional intelligence seek success for the whole group and are willing to change their own interests and whims for the whole team. They are good empathetic listeners with the ability to read people's emotions and feelings. They do not judge immediately as well. They try to put themselves in other people's shoes before reaching a resolution to a conflict in relationships.

The above attributes make emotionally intelligent people good at managing people and relationships.

Emotional Intelligence and Leadership

Surely, fine and exceptional skills are valuable assets in an organization. It is difficult to ignore a person with shameless brilliance and brilliant talent. However, the criterion for a good leader goes beyond skill and talent. To stay in an organization, a person needs a lot of emotional intelligence. This is very true, especially if the person aspires to lead an organization one day. The leader has many responsibilities that need more than just skill and talent. All the responsibilities that come with leadership can only be carried out well if the leader is equipped with emotional intelligence.

Leadership is a social activity. Leaders need

to nurture their emotional intelligence continuously to be able to deal with different types of personalities in an organization.

Emotional intelligence is usually equated with "people skills". Emotional intelligence is not just about people skills, although a lot of emotional intelligence is needed to sharpen people skills. Leadership requires forming and maintaining relationships with various personalities. Only a leader with high emotional intelligence can forge strong relationships with his or her team and maintain them. A high emotional intelligence will allow a leader to relate to various personalities and still motivate each team member to fulfill the objective of the organization.

Leadership requires emotional intelligence,

especially in times of conflict and pressure. Conflicts and problems arise from all kinds of angles. Internal conflict can arise from people in the organization fighting with each other. In order to handle such problems, a leader needs emotional intelligence to keep emotions under control. In times of extreme pressure, leaders must be able to avoid explosive outbursts. A good leader must be able to put things in perspective rather than succumb to emotional outbursts. Managing a team of diverse personalities is manageable when a leader has the right amount of emotional intelligence. An empathetic leader who is considerate of all team members has enough emotional intelligence to confront troubled members of the organization without breaking relationships. Emotional intelligence on the leader's side will allow him/her to help the problem member express his/her feelings in a healthy way.

Decision-making is another leadership task that requires immense emotional intelligence. There will be many factors that affect a leader's decision, including external factors, criticism and unforeseen situations. A leader with emotional intelligence will have the good sense to weigh the pros and cons of any situation before making a decision. Leaders with emotional intelligence have enough ability to make quick, well thought-out decisions. Leaders must be emotionally intelligent in order to make independent decisions, without being influenced by unnecessary factors. Emotional intelligence is needed to see clearly and objectively strengths and weaknesses, especially one's own. Leaders need a good look at their assets and weaknesses in order to make a decision and eventually follow through.

THE BIG LEADER LEADERSHIP EXPERT

Exercising and improving one's emotional intelligence for leadership

Emotional intelligence can develop and improve over time. One of the first steps would be to practice self-awareness in managing stress.

Recognizing the various emotions you feel when you are under pressure and stress will make it easier to deal with them. By being aware of the various emotions that run through a person's head, he or she will easily understand the emotions before they dominate his or her thoughts, words, and actions. Self-awareness is about recognizing one's own feelings and thoughts, but it can be developed with the help of others. Seek feedback from the people around you - supervisors, colleagues, etc. It is also important to get feedback from other people in order to recognize the impact of your emotions and actions on other people. This is important to improve the dynamics and relationship of each member. If the leader can practice self-awareness, he or she can set a good example for the whole team.

Part of self-awareness knows your strengths and weaknesses. You cannot be too humble to downplay your strengths; this is simply false humility. An emotionally intelligent leader needs to understand the importance of recognizing efforts without showing off. On the other hand, one cannot be too arrogant about achievements and strengths. A complete self-evaluation of one's strengths and weaknesses requires courage and honesty. In relation to self-awareness, one can also begin to improve emotional intelligence through self-reflection. Notice how you react to certain situations, especially stressful ones. Do you break easily with an attack? Do you hit your colleagues easily? These are the things you need to evaluate because they are all part of your emotional intelligence.

Improving your emotional intelligence means broadening your threshold for stressful situations, whether it is an internal conflict in the organization or a large amount of work. These things really do have their way of taking their toll on a person, but they are actually things that determine a person's emotional intelligence. A leader who lacks emotional intelligence will walk away and succumb to these challenges. In the midst of all these challenges, do not just wave your white flag immediately. Don't give up on stressful situations without thinking about it. Learn to be aware of your own thoughts when facing these situations and to control them. Put your emotions in order and distance yourself from them so you can put things in perspective. Ask yourself: "What can I do and what can't I do?" Look at the problem in terms of the solutions you can provide and let go of the things that have no solutions. Focus your energies on the things that can be remedied.

When dealing with problematic colleagues and workers, don't let your emotions guide your decisions and actions. Most of the time, a career is destroyed by defective relationships with colleagues and subordinates. Don't launch personal diatribes against the person. If you have a tendency to explode immediately, walk away from the problem first and vent your anger without lashing out at the person. What part of the problem is the person's fault? Is there something that could have been done on their behalf? Are other people involved? Don't focus too much on the person. Instead, address the problem. When you have put things in perspective, talk to the person but listen to their side first. Listen to their points of view without prejudice, judgments and stereotypes. Empathy is very important at this time. It is important as a leader, especially when making decisions regarding your team members involved in the conflict.

Even if one of the team members is at fault, it is your job as a leader to make sure that the culprit acknowledges his or her faults without feeling judged. This is an indicator of how much emotional intelligence a leader has.

Chapter 4: Building Successful Teams and Relationships

If you want to build successful relationships with your people, you have to be able to project yourself as more than just a person with authority. People need to respect you, not fear you. In the previous chapter, empathy and emotional intelligence were discussed at length. You will need to use these two to establish a stable foundation for your relationships with your team members. It also starts with having a good relationship with yourself. This means getting to know yourself, your strengths and weaknesses, your potential for improvement and how you react in various situations. Once you become familiar with your personality, dealing with other people's personalities would be manageable.

In addition, part of building a successful relationship with your team is discovering what motivates each of them so they can be more productive and ultimately find personal growth and fulfillment on their own.

One of the duties of the leader is to make the entire organization constantly productive. Productivity is certainly important in an organization that seeks a competitive and successful advantage. Productivity is based on individual and team effort, both of which can be addressed through team building. Team building is supposed to produce a group of individuals working together to execute different tasks. It takes confidence and strong team dynamics to execute these tasks.

What makes a team strong? A strong team must have a common goal. A team can be made up of members who perform different functions but they must always have a primary goal in order to call themselves a team. Team members are supposed to perform the tasks assigned to them, but they must rely to some extent on other members to achieve the common goal. They will help each other if necessary to achieve the common goals. Even if they have individual goals, their individual goals should be aligned with the common goals. Cooperation must be rooted in each member of the team at all times.

Team building sessions should establish the goals of the team, recognize the problems that prevent the team from achieving those goals, and propose ways for the entire team to achieve those goals. Guidelines exist for establishing team building sessions, but how each session is designed still depends on the size and nature of the organization. For example, project-based teams tend to change their composition constantly. Given these circumstances, team building activities should focus on the skills of each individual that will enable him or her to become an effective team member. In a team where the members are relatively permanent, the focus will shift to how each team member relates to the others. How team members relate to each other will have a direct impact on their productivity. Therefore, the nature of the team should be examined before designing a team-building session.

The goal of planning for team building should be to make each team member aware of the seriousness of his or her tasks. Each member should also know why he or she is participating in the organization. At the end of team building, they should be reminded of their purpose in the organization.

When planning team building activities, make sure that there are activities that are related to the tasks that people normally perform. It does not have to be a completely technical skill, but activities that facilitate team dynamics while employing their skills. For example, marketing executives can participate in a team building activity where they organize themselves into teams and are given a certain amount of money to buy certain things. They have to adjust the budget without compromising the quality of their items and time constraints. In the end, participants have to realize that they have to think like their customers.

In addition, working on this activity in groups will encourage productive brainstorming.

Team building activities should also focus on conflict resolution. Although a chapter will be assigned for this, it is worth discussing conflict resolution in terms of team building. Different types of conflicts will plague team members and threaten their relationship. Each member must be equipped with the skills necessary to manage conflict to ensure a harmonious relationship between themselves, their leaders and the people they regularly deal with.

Conflict is not the total ruin of an organization. It can facilitate the generation of brilliant ideas and the strengthening of relationships, as long as the conflict is well managed.

One of the most sensible ways to manage conflict is to improve the lines of communication between members of the organization. You may want to divide your team into pairs and let each pair stand back to back. One person should hold a paper and pencil while the other holds an image in a (definite or abstract) way. The person holding the image should describe the shape to the person with the pencil and paper, giving as much detail as possible. The pairs are given a time limit. Once the timer is turned off, the pairs should compare their representation with the original shape. How did the person with the picture describe the shape? Was it well described? Did the person with the paper and pencil draw the picture accurately enough? Were there any communication problems? These are the questions that conflict resolution should address.

Conflicts often arise from a lack of trust, a great killer of team spirit. If you are conducting a team building seminar in a large space, you can do this activity. To do this, spread objects with obstacles (e.g., cones, chairs, boxes, blocks, tables) around the room. Again, assign the team in pairs.

As a leader, take note that this activity is geared toward solving trust issues.

Therefore, you may want to group two people who have difficulty trusting each other. Blindly bend one person and keep the other person out of the "obstacle zone. Put the blindfolded person in the middle of the area and let the other person give the blindfolded person instructions on how to get out of that area. The blindfolded person cannot speak or talk under any circumstances. The blindfolded person should avoid obstacles in his or her way out. Let each pair strategize for a few minutes before starting, but only about how to communicate during the game. Do not let them see the area.

Leaders should facilitate solidarity, even outside of team building sessions. As a leader, you must be able to identify if there are any barriers that prevent people from working together. Some teams, especially large ones, tend to divide into small groups and teams. Leaders must be able to follow up on these things and recognize the cause, whether it is insignificant or serious. Sometimes the cause can be as insignificant as different departmental dress codes. If this is the cause of the conflict, there should be a dress code imposed on all team members.

This phenomenon is very common in large organizations (e.g. the marketing department conflict with the human resources department, a branch office complains about the central office, etc.). Leaders in management positions would be tempted to host a corporate social function to eradicate these boundaries, but this plan can be counterproductive if not properly planned. For example, at a casual corporate picnic where all employees are invited, they might continue to seek out their friends and resort to cliques. Worse still, this can start a fight since all employees are in one place.

If you want to improve relationships between members or co-workers, you can start by identifying barriers or markers that divide people before bringing them together at a team-building session or social function. List the specific conflicts between the team and resolve them with the people involved. For example, cliques in the office might be caused by language and cultural barriers. FI this is the case, you may occasionally group people of different races together for certain tasks.

Encourage transparency and honesty in the different departments, but also very technical. Sometimes the gap gets bigger when two different groups are assigned to work with each other, but one of them uses jargon terms when talking to non-experts. Discourage this attitude among employees, especially technical staff.

Team members are more likely to have strong relationships with each other if they have a good relationship with their leader. As your team builds relationships, guide and monitor them accordingly. Knowing that they have a leader they can consult and understand will make them feel confident and secure in building relationships with their peers.

Team building is a continuous process. Determining your success is not done in a single session. And, any organization that seeks to stay in shape should always seek to strengthen its teams. This cannot be done in a single team building session. In the end, leaders must remember that team building is a long-term process. People usually join an organization in the hope of staying as long as possible, seeking growth and self-realization.

With this in mind, the leader must make a point of establishing team building as a continuous and permanent process. It is useless to establish a team building process just to return to normal activities as if team building activities had never been done. Over time, team building activities should be modified according to the competencies, strengths and weaknesses of the members. Team building activities should be planned in relation to the outcomes of previous team building sessions. It should never be assumed that successful team building does not stop with a single session. Teams and organizational relationships must be constantly nurtured if they are to remain progressive and stable at the same time.

Chapter 5: Managing Difficult Times and Conflict Effectively

Even the best leaders are forced to find obstacles along the way. In fact, leaders do not have it easy because their position puts them under constant public scrutiny. Every mistake they make is magnified, and sometimes leaders feel like they are being pulled in all directions. Mistakes are inevitable because leadership is a learning process. You make mistakes, learn from them and rise above them.

It is always good to prepare when you get into something - hobby, career, activity, etc.

Leadership is no different. In leadership, there are some points to remember to prepare you to face the pitfalls.

One of the pitfalls leaders must avoid is lack of concentration.

Leadership does not mean that you take on all the tasks or that you are required to know everything. As a leader, it is your job to motivate your team and streamline all activities to achieve a common goal. It is your job to lead your team in the right direction. Your team will admire and trust you to lead it. You can ask them to do some things on their own but it is your duty as a leader to provide them with direction. It's easy to lose sight of the goal because as a leader, you will be undertaking a diverse set of tasks. Often, it is easy to lose focus in the midst of all these tasks. Leaders should always remember that before executing a task or facilitating an activity, they must ensure that they are aligned with the common end goal.

The second obstacle is dangerous. Many aspiring leaders begin with the promise of serving rather than being served and putting the welfare of others ahead of their own. But staying up there is difficult in terms of managing power. Power can make a leader drunk. Leaders enjoy privilege and prestige. When you're at the top, you can easily sneak in your own agenda and put it ahead of the whole group. Leaders should avoid this trap because while it may seem glamorous at first, it will eventually be destructive to the entire organization. When the organization falls apart, it is the leader who usually takes the first blame. Putting oneself first in their priorities is especially tempting in difficult

times. Corrupt politicians fall into this trap. However, they do not usually enjoy a happy ending. There is a lot of serfdom in leadership. Always put your organization and your cause above your personal agenda.

Good leaders have the eyes of a hawk when it comes to details. They make sure that all the loose ends are tied up and the little problems are solved. This is certainly a good trait but if this goes too far, there may be a tendency for the leader to micromanage the smallest and most unnecessary things. As mentioned earlier, leaders should not do all the tasks on their teams. In fact, there may be some technical things that the leader or manager may not be aware of. Sometimes a leader has to let things go in order to focus on more important things. When leaders focus too much on unnecessary details, they lose sight of the big picture. This also puts them at risk of losing focus, which leads them back to the first problem. Leaders need to learn what the important things are so they know what to focus on.

Because leaders are supposed to lead the whole team, there is a notion that leaders are infallible. Sometimes, this goes to the head of some leaders.

When they make a mistake or a bad decision, they may take it personally or refuse to acknowledge it. Both reactions are unhealthy because in reality, leaders can still make mistakes. Leadership is a learning process.

Not everything you know initially will apply to your context. You have to make adjustments to your judgments. Sometimes you only realize this when you make mistakes. Mistakes should naturally be avoided, but once they are there, they should be acknowledged. Leaders must accept their mistakes in order to learn from them and make better decisions next time.

Leaders will encounter problems they may not have encountered before. Some of these problems may be only slight variations of the problems they normally encounter.

Others are completely different, something for which they have no immediate solutions. No matter how new these problems are, leaders must always be prepared to adapt to any situation for the survival of their organization. Conferences, seminars and workshops will only come to a point. However, they will not provide solutions to all problems. Great leaders have the ability to cope with the unpredictable circumstances that befall them.

The ability to embrace change is the essential weapon of any leader to steer the organization in the right direction, even if they lose sight of their path along the way.

Leaders need common sense, creativity and ingenuity to adapt to unpredictable circumstances. In addition, part of adapting to change is letting go of ineffective mindsets. Good leaders trust the conventional structure, but they also know when to let go when it does not work in certain circumstances. Leaders must be critical of both old and new mentalities to constantly seek better ways of doing things.

Lack of communication is another common problem that leaders will encounter. Even the most experienced are not spared. New leaders face communication problems because they are still familiarizing themselves with their teams. Experienced leaders may encounter communication problems when they become too complacent and refuse to listen to their team, thinking they already know how to handle matters. The success of an organization depends largely on the interaction of its members.

Given changing times and unpredictable circumstances, the sure way to manage the dynamics of an organization is to keep the lines of communication open and unbiased as much as possible. Leaders should seek to establish to their team that, although they may not always agree with all of their members, they remain accessible and open to communicative dialogue.

Strong and respectable leadership does not mean that challenges and obstacles do not arise. It simply means that the leader has the right skills to overcome those obstacles. In fact, it is those obstacles that determine whether or not the leader deserves the privileges and responsibilities.

Conflict management/ management of conflicts

In conflict management, open lines of communication are your medicine and reliable preventive remedy. Even before conflicts arise, leaders must already create an environment in which everyone is free to express his or her mind in the most appropriate and respectful manner. Leaders must encourage healthy discussions during meetings and even in casual conversations. This includes all members of the organization, regardless of age, sex, race and rank.

Even if there are disagreements, respect should not be lost in discussions. Everyone should be encouraged to adjust to each other's differences.

When conflict already exists, leaders should take the first step to identify and understand the root of the conflict. No harsh judgments should be made until all parties are heard. Leaders should also emphasize that the goal of understanding the conflict is to resolve it, not to make it big. All parties involved should be encouraged to set their sights on resolution, not on a major conflict. Encourage healthy conflict resolution to improve and strengthen group dynamics, increase mutual respect and gain a better perspective on the common goals of the company.

In conflict resolution, leaders should be cautious about playing the blame game. They can do so by separating the person from the problem. One person may cause a problem but this does not give anyone (including the leader) the right to accuse the person of being the problem. Leaders who can separate the problems from the people will avoid doing permanent damage to the relationship.

Listening is a primary component in conflict resolution. The leader must understand where each side is coming from. They must be given the right to defend their own position without offending the other party. In the process, the leader must facilitate the clarification of facts. Objectivity is required from the leader as a facilitator. At the same time, he must listen to the interests of each side. This will give a better view of why the parties involved are taking such sides.

Once all parties have expressed themselves, the leader should consolidate all the information presented and clarify all the facts presented to all. A resolution cannot be formed if not everyone agrees with the facts. Summarize the statements of each side and clarify their feelings.

Once everyone agrees on the problem, everyone can think of possible solutions.

Leaders should keep in mind that there are different ways to solve a problem. Most of the time, all the parties involved have to be committed to meet halfway. There are times when the position of the other party really has to become unpopular, especially if that position steps on someone in some way. There are also solutions that give all parties what they want without the risk of another conflict. Leaders have their own styles of resolving conflict. There are leaders who try to avoid conflict altogether while there are some who face the problem head on to end it. Whatever the style, it must also fit the problem at hand.

When the resolution has been negotiated, the leader and the parties involved must find ways to prevent the conflict in the future. This should also build stronger relationships between colleagues.

Leaders should not fear conflict, as it can present opportunities to reassess objectives and strengthen relationships. As long as the leader is armed with strong conflict management skills, he or she should not be a source of harmful tension.

Visit our author page on Amazon and get more MENTES LIBRES!

http://amazon.com/author/menteslibres

If you wish, you can leave a comment on this book by clicking on the following link so that we can continue to grow! Thank you very much for your purchase!

https://www.amazon.com/dp/B084L5M451

www.ingramcontent.com/pod-product-compliance
Lightning Source LLC
Chambersburg PA
CBHW050254220526
45465CB00002B/673